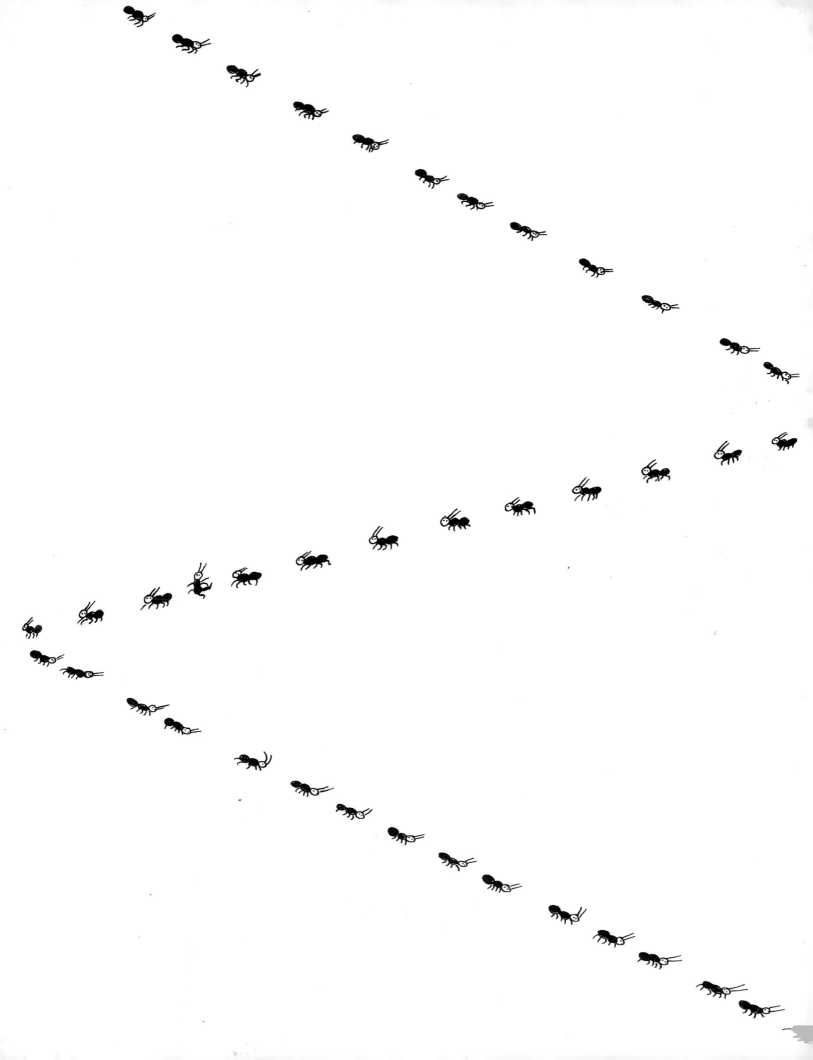

TO NICHOLAS STEPHEN WALTON,
WHO'S CUTER THAN A BUG
R.W.

TO JIMMY,
A BUG LOVER
N.C.

The illustrations in this book were done in magic markers on
watercolor paper. The display type was set in Bertram. The
text was set in ITC Kabel. Separations by Colotone Graphics.
Printed and bound by Berryville Graphics
Production supervision by Esilda Kerr

Library of Congress Cataloging in Publication Data was not
available in time for the publication of this book,
but can be obtained from the Library of Congress.
What To Do When A Bug Climbs In Your Mouth
And Other Poems To Drive You Buggy.
ISBN 0-688-13658-3. ISBN 0-688-13659-1 (lib. bdg.).
Library of Congress Catalog Card Number 94-79124.

WHAT TO DO WHEN
A BUG CLIMBS
IN YOUR MOUTH

AND OTHER POEMS TO DRIVE YOU BUGGY

BY RICK WALTON

PICTURES BY NANCY CARLSON

LOTHROP, LEE & SHEPARD BOOKS   NEW YORK

What to Do When a Bug Climbs in Your Mouth

When a bug climbs in your mouth
and you don't know what to do

Metamorphosis

I watched an ugly caterpillar
wrap itself in green,
then turn into the prettiest little
thing I've ever seen.

I wrapped myself in blankets that were
on my closet shelf.
And when I took them off—
I was still my ugly self.

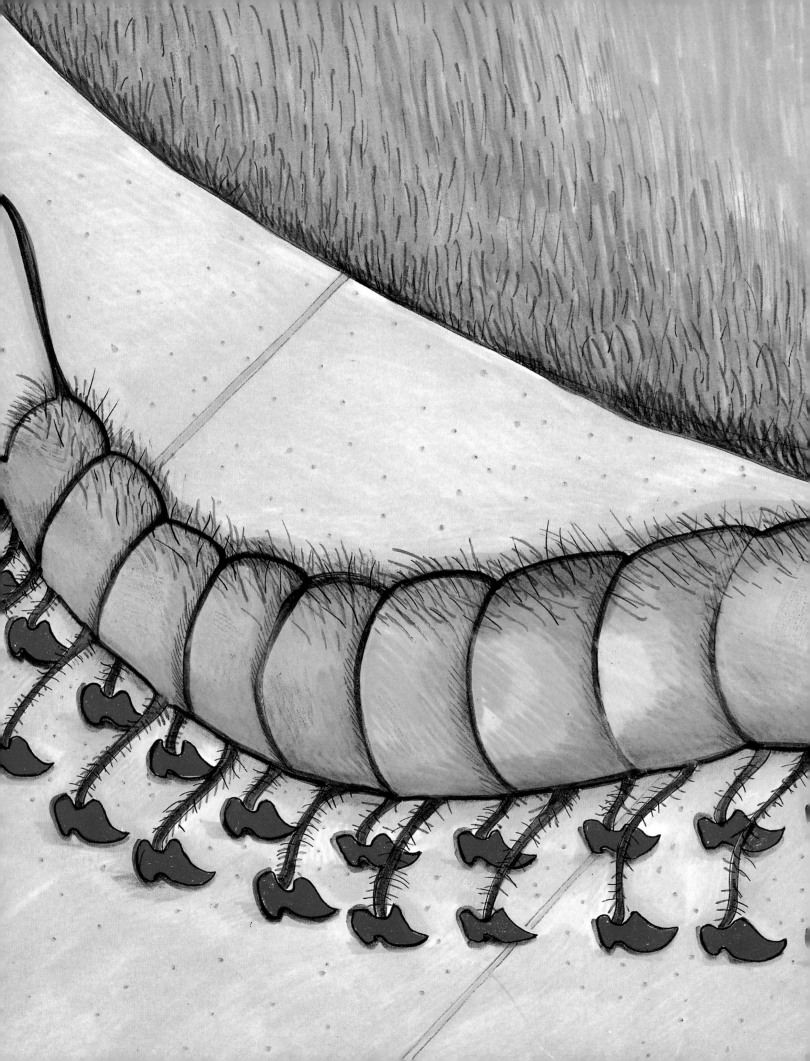

Clickety-Clock

A centipede came down the walk,
clickety-clock, clickety-clock.
"What makes your feet go clickety-clock
as you go strolling down the walk?"
I asked the bug. And he replied,
"The shoes I put my feet inside.
They're made of wood — the shoes, that is.
They're from my uncle. They were his
until the day he grew those bunions
while he walked through fields of onions.
But I'm off now, must be going;
I'm afraid it might start snowing
and my snowshoes are all hung
at home. They need to be restrung.
Good-bye, it was so nice to talk."
And off he hurried down the walk,
clickety-clock, clickety-clock.

Billions of Bugs

There are bugs in your carpet
and bugs in your hair.
There are millions
and billions
of bugs everywhere.
They will eat up your trees,
they will dig up your lawn.
You can squash all you can,
but they'll never be gone.
They will dive in your food.
They will hide in your bed.
You will never get rid
of your bugs.
          So instead—
Ask them kindly
not to bite.
Do not wash them
from your hair.
Let them know
you'll treat them right.
Learn to love them.
Show you care.

You might as well—
They're everywhere.

In My Lunch Box

There's a grasshopper sandwich
for me today!
(I hope that the inside
hasn't hopped away.)

What Would You Do?

If a bug
were on the sidewalk,
would you feed it?
would you wash it?
or would you be naughty and
squash it?

The History of the Cockroach

A million gazillion years ago
the first cockroach hatched and said, "Hello!"

"Hello there," it said to the rocks and the trees.
"Hello" to the fishes that crept from the seas.

"Hello" to the dinosaurs stomping the ground.
"Hello!" to the people when they came around.

And someday when all of us finally die,
the cockroach will be there to tell us, "Good-bye!"

And after it sheds a few small cockroach tears,
it will live for a million gazillion more years.

Bug Catcher

I tried to catch a ladybug,
  but she hid on a strawberry
  and I couldn't find her.

I tried to catch a caterpillar,
  but she crawled onto a ball of yarn
  and disappeared.

I tried to catch a butterfly,
  but she landed on a flower
  and I couldn't see her.

I tried to catch a cricket,
  but he jumped into a pile of coal
  and was gone.

I tried to catch a fly,
  but he hid himself
  on a slice of watermelon.

Bugs are just too smart for me.

I Do

Onto the tip of the top of the tap
comes the ant.
He tries to curl up and take a nap
but he can't.
He slithers, he slides, he slips, he falls.
And as he falls, he sees me and calls,
"Oh, catch me, please, or I am through!"

I do.

Bee Song

The bumblebee's a little thing
who loves to sing, and sing, and sing.
And if you don't applaud his song,
he'll sting!

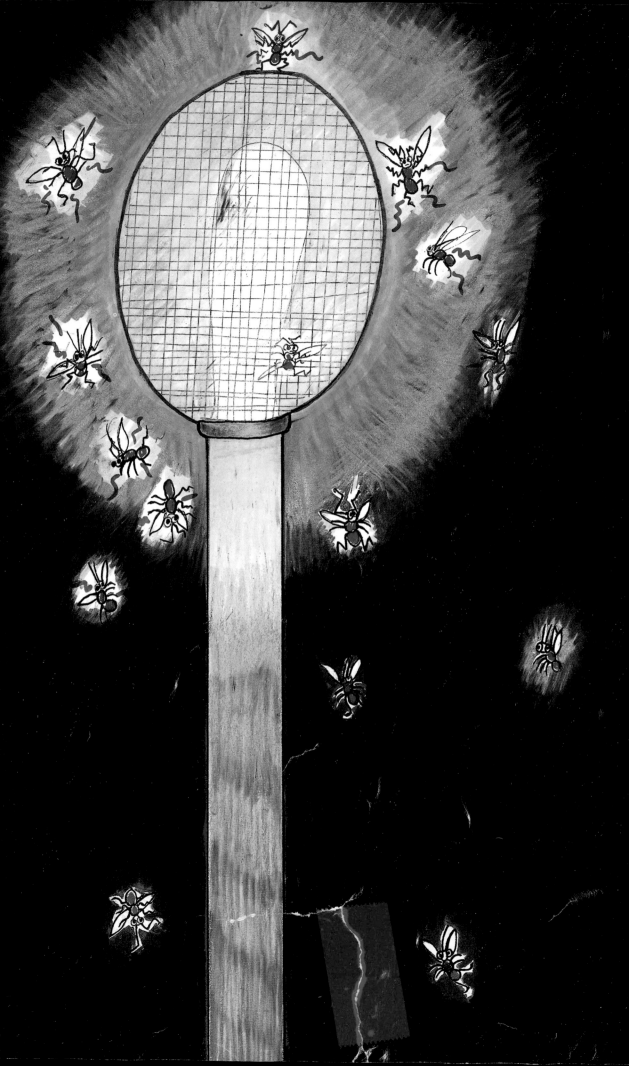

Bug Zapper

Gnats are not new,
they were bothering Noah.
You find them in Pittsburgh,
Morocco, and Goa.
They fly in your mouth,
up your nose, in your eye.
How I love it when I
hear those little things fry.

The Early Worm

The early bird has caught his prey
and now the worm is dead,
which goes to show that smarter worms
are those who stay in bed.

Let's Spray

To all of you bugs
who eat my fruit:
STOP, OR I'LL SHOOT!

Four Nevers

Never eat a cockroach whole
unless it climbs into your bowl.

Never open up a jar
of bumblebees while in a car.

Never bite a worm in two
unless a whole's too big to chew.

Never open up a can
of army ants while in a van.

So Let That Be a Lesson to You!

"My goodness!" said the gadfly
as he gobbled down his dinner.
"All I do is eat and eat,
and all I get is thin and thinner.
Think, my thinker, why the thinning
with such stuff inside my inner?
Must be something in my doing,
and the doing must be dinner."

So the gadfly gave up dinner
and his lunch and breakfast, too.
Now with nothing in his inner
this old gadfly looked like new.
Fat and sassy, full of flavor,
now the gadfly, proud and stirred,
flew too high and flew too mighty
and was pecked up by a bird.

Insect Questions

If you shake a milkweed plant,
do you get butterflies?

If you shake a kingsize milkweed plant,
do you get monarch butterflies?

Do carpenter ants
build houseflies?

If a firefly caught a housefly on fire,
would a water bug put out the housefly?

Do dragonflies breathe fireflies?

If a dragonfly
kidnapped a queen bee,
would the monarch butterfly
send knight crawlers
to rescue her?

The Dance

The elephant asked the handsome ant
if he would like to dance.
He said, "Of course!" They tripped and clomped
and basked in their romance.

But she was clumsy, he was slow.
She smashed him underneath her toe.
And when she saw him there, she said,
"Oh, what an awful blow!"

Busy Busy Busy

I'm a busy, busy, busy, busy
bumblebee,
and there's no one who is busier
than busy, busy me.
I don't know what I am doing,
but as you can see,
I'm a busy, busy, busy, busy
bumblebee.

Beetle Rancheros

Underneath the oak tree,
beneath the lowest branch,
a butterfly and bumblebee
run a beetle ranch.

They rope 'em and they brand 'em,
and they sell 'em by the bunch
to schools like yours who put 'em in
the food they serve for lunch.

Slug Bug Cheer

Give me an S!
Give me an L!
Give me a   U!
Give me a   G!
Give me a SLUG!
Give me a SLUG!
Give me a SLUG SLUG SLUG!

OUCH! NOT THAT KIND!